The Private World *of* KATHARINE HEPBURN

The Private World of KATHARINE HEPBURN

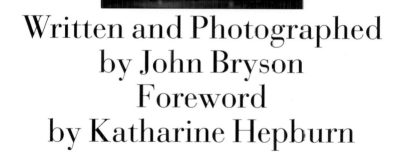

Written and Photographed
by John Bryson
Foreword
by Katharine Hepburn

Little, Brown and Company Boston Toronto London

Designed by Will Hopkins

to Nancy,
who makes it all possible,
and Norman

ACKNOWLEDGMENTS

THE BOOK:
Will Hopkins, gentleman, artist, and dear friend.
Stephen Brewer, protector and polisher of each sacred word.
Bill Phillips, editor enthusiasticus.

SOME PREDECESSORS:
The LIFE editors and Harry Luce, who brought me out of the Texas
wilderness eons ago, and especially LIFE editors Ed Thompson,
Philip Kunhardt, Richard Stolley, Hugh Moffett, Frank McCulloch.

MAGAZINES THAT RAN KATE HEPBURN STORIES AND COVERS:
LIFE, TIME, PEOPLE, NEWSWEEK, LADIES' HOME JOURNAL,
THE LONDON SUNDAY TIMES, PARIS MATCH, MS., MCCALL'S,
HARPER'S BAZAAR, ARCHITECTURAL DIGEST, NEW YORK, ETC.

PEOPLE WITH US, OR DEPARTED, WHO ENRICHED THE JOURNEY:
Elli Katzenstein, John Durniak, John Huston, Sam Peckinpah,
Robert Mitchum, Michael Rand, Alfred Eisenstaedt, Indio Fernandez,
Amanda 'Binky' Urban.

AND ALSO:
Kate Hepburn and Nancy Bryson, than which there ain't no others.
–John Bryson

First Paperback Edition

Library of Congress Cataloging-in-Publication Data
Bryson, John.
    The private world of Katharine Hepburn / photographs by
John Bryson; foreword by Katharine Hepburn. — 1st ed.
     p. cm.
    ISBN 0-316-11332-8 (hc)
    ISBN 0-316-11333-6 (pb)
    1. Hepburn, Katharine. 1909– —Portraits. I. Title
PN2287.H45B79   1990
791.43'028'092—dc20   90-5490
                           CIP

10 9 8 7 6 5 4 3 2 1

Published simultaneously in Canada
by Little, Brown & Company (Canada) Limited

Designer: Will Hopkins, Hopkins/Baumann
Design Associates: Joseph Lee, Robert Lesser,
Wylie Nash
Production Associate: Jane McFadden
Editorial Associates: Stephen Brewer, Amy Hughes,
Mitchell Nauffts, Cynthia Sophiea

The text and layout for this book were produced entirely on Macintosh
computers employing Aldus Pagemaker, Adobe Illustrator, and Microsoft
Word. The typefaces are Bauer Bodoni, Bodoni, and Bodoni Book from the
Adobe Type Library.

Printed in Japan

Pictures, pictures, pictures…
"Listen, Kate, can I…well, what are you doing today?"
"What am I doing? How the hell do I know what I'm doing? Oh, John, no…."
"Well, I'm coming up there…I've got an idea."
And then two and a half hours later he'd walk into the Fenwick house….
"Oh, John…I was just going for a bike ride…."
"Well, why not…. Wait, I'll get my stuff…."
His stuff…you know what that is. His camera. His flash. Well, his equipment for
taking all these pictures that you're about to look at.

John has been following me around.
I don't mean that I'm the only one he's following around.
But on the slightest provocation…yes, that's right…taking pictures.
On a bicycle…in a boat…in a tree…in the snow…in the water…in a movie…
at a wedding…laughing…crying…Yes, he's there.
Well, you know…I mean…if I'm there…he's there.
And it finally gets to be kind of fun.
And years pass…and you look at these pictures….
They bring back so many memories…so many thoughts…so many things….
The places…the trees…the flowers…the happies…the furies…
the no-longer-with-us memories.
Photographs have become a real part of our lives.
And of course in a way they are my life.
I am a sort of sight and sound photo…much more than the real me.

A man … a man about 70…looked at me today.
We were both at a church fair in Old Saybrook.
(No, John wasn't there, for once.)
"Oh, you," he said. "Don't I know you? Yes? No? Do I?"
He looked hard.
"Well, I don't know," I said.
"Oh…oh…that voice…that sound…Aren't you…?"
"Yes, I suppose I am," I said. "You mean Katharine…?
Yes. Yes, I'm Katharine…."
"Yes…of course you are…. You look like her."

Well, here she is…the one you know…I mean that Katharine….
– *Katharine Hepburn, New York, Spring 1990*

PREFACE

I FIRST MET and photographed Katharine Hepburn in 1974 on an Oregon movie location for LIFE magazine.

I was certainly not a journalistic virgin when I encountered her. I had previously had the fortune to photograph, with some intimacy, such figures as Ernest Hemingway, William Faulkner, Salvador Dali, Norman Rockwell, Presidents Dwight Eisenhower, John Kennedy (I did his campaign posters), Lyndon Johnson, Richard Nixon, and Jimmy Carter, General Franco, King Juan Carlos, the Shah of Iran, Nikita Khrushchev, General MacArthur, directors John Huston, Sam Peckinpah, and Cecil B. DeMille, Orson Welles, Marilyn Monroe, Marlene Dietrich, Humphrey Bogart, Lauren Bacall, Elizabeth Taylor, James Stewart, Yul Brynner, Mary Pickford, Sir Laurence Olivier, Jason Robards, Robert Mitchum, Louis Armstrong, Frank Sinatra, Lee Marvin, Clint Eastwood. Name-droppers of the world, unite. But there *were* a lot of predecessors.

However, there has been no one, before or after, like Katharine Houghton Hepburn. Mean as a snake, dear as an angel, she is one of the great humans, better than the legend. She is *all* that she appears to be, with a face for Mount Rushmore.

Six months after the Oregon meeting, I was assigned by another magazine to photograph her at her Beverly Hills house (14 rolls of Kodachrome says my appointments calendar); eight months later I did her in New York for another publication; and after that, through the years, anytime the opportunity presented itself I photographed her, at homes, movie locations, theatrical productions, all over.

She does not suffer fools easily, and I was flattered by her friendship. We both hate posed pictures, so *that* worked well. She serves good drinks and the best beet soup in the world but she hates my jokes. She can be a virago when one is late but then she gives that Hepburn smile and says, "My father would drive off without us if we weren't on time, so I'm practically always early. I'm very, very conscious of being late."

Unknowingly, she improved my lifestyle: My answering-service ladies in New York and California would go into paroxysms as they advised me, "Katharine Hepburn called. It was really her, I recognized her voice. She was so gracious." I ended up having maybe the best answering-service treatment in the world.

Initially there was never any thought of a book like this. But I began to notice that my Hepburn files did contain a remarkable variety of pictures, and so in 1981 I brought them to the editor of LIFE, Phil Kunhardt. He ran 12 pages of pictures with the title, THE PRIVATE WORLD OF KATHARINE HEPBURN. Obviously, that is when the book soup began to simmer, though it went on simmering for the next nine years.

At the time of the LIFE story Kunhardt interviewed her to find out why she had let me into the privacy of her life—doing the family house in Connecticut for the first time and all—had I worn her down?

"It's about time it got photographed," she said. "These things work both ways. I don't get worn down unless I feel like it."

But why, he asked, of all the photographers who had approached her over the years, had she opened up to John Bryson?

Her answer: "I just like him. I trust him."

That might make me a hell of an epitaph.

—John Bryson

FENWICK

◆ At the house in Fenwick, she stands in the driveway with her hand-painted plea to be left alone. "People in Fenwick respect my privacy," she says. "I'm nothing special to them, you know. Apparently some of the children think it's rather romantic that I'm here, but the ones of my generation don't think anything about it."

◆ She climbs her own trees and does her own pruning, sawing, cleaning up, and disposal—she would never hire a gardener.

KATHARINE HOUGHTON HEPBURN, one of six children of Dr. and Mrs. Thomas Norval Hepburn, was born on November 8, 1909, a date that is sometimes disputed. She grew up in Hartford, Connecticut. Her Virginia-born father was one of the leading urologists in the country and her mother a leading proponent of women's rights before the idea had gained acceptance. She spent much of her youth alternating between home and the family country retreat, also in Connecticut, on the shores of Long Island Sound at Fenwick.

She has gone on to make 42 motion pictures, for which she received 12 Academy Award nominations for Best Actress, and she has won four Oscars, an all-time record. She has never attended the Academy Awards ceremonies to accept the Oscar statuettes, and she has never displayed them in her home. In between films, she has appeared in at least 25 stage productions, from early young walk-ons to Broadway smashes and triumphant Shakespearean vehicles all over the world, as well as six major television movies.

"Some people are very lucky, and have been endowed," she says. "Look at me. People say I've worked hard. I *have* worked hard, but my God, haven't I been lucky? Good health, good inheritance, wonderful parents, the whole thing.

"Mother was very feminine, very quick, very sharp, a brilliant speaker, a wonderful debater, yet it was Dad who got Mother involved in women's suffrage. He felt she was getting a little bored, so he persuaded her to come to a lecture given by that militant suffragist Emmeline Pankhurst, a tiny, charming woman. She and Mother became close friends. Dad used to be great at writing all the signs and things for the suffrage parades. My first public appearance was carrying a flag in one of those parades and my first real, thrilling job was filling balloons with gas, then tying strings around them and making people buy them. The balloons all said, 'VOTES FOR WOMEN.'

"My older brother died when he was

◆ Overleaf: Her father bought the Fenwick house around 1910, and she was there when the hurricane of 1938 devastated much of coastal New England. The house was rebuilt, and her brother Richard, a writer, lives there year round. Here, Kate and Dick set off in a canoe rigged for sailing, her favorite craft.

◆ She drags tree limbs up the driveway where she will cut them into firewood for Fenwick and her house in New York.

◆ The horticultural Hepburn is a legend even among old-time Fenwickians.

◆ Almost every week-
end, with secretary
Phyllis Wilbourn in
tow, Kate makes the
three-hour drive
from New York to
Fenwick. She spends
much of her week-
ends doing house-
work; here, she buffs
the dining-room
table.

◆ Parcheesi fan
Hepburn (top) enjoys
a game with Dick,
Phyllis, and friend
Virginia Harrington.

◆ Kate visits with
younger sister Peg at
her farm in Canton
Center, Connecticut.

◆ "This is the great movie star doing the laundry," says Kate, as she lays things out to dry on the lawn in front of Long Island Sound.

nearly 16 and I was 13, and this tragedy threw my mother and father and me very close together. I was conscious of them as people because they were young. Usually kids think of their parents as middle-aged people. And I was conscious of them as friends, and I was equally close to both of them. Unusual, yes. When we would speak together, it was a very different conversation from what they would have had with anyone else. I think every human relationship requires a tremendous amount of work to make it go, really. Our relationship was very, very close because they made it close. So did I. Whenever I needed them, they were there. They were a source of infinite strength."

Every weekend she drives the three hours from her Manhattan town house and spends several days in the old digs. "The me I know is the person at Fenwick," she says. Her immediate family is in the area: brother Robert, 75, a retired surgeon, lives nearby; younger sister Peg, a librarian, is about an hour away; her sister Marion died several years ago, but her brother-in-law has a house in Fenwick; and the countryside is filled with nieces and nephews.

"I'm like the girl who never grew up, you see. I just never left home, so to speak. I've always come back. I've come back almost every weekend of my life. I've had the New York house since 1931 but I don't suppose I've spent ten weekends there."

◆ She walks through the woods near the house, enjoying the Queen Anne's lace (her favorite flower) of her beloved Fenwick. "This is the real me," she says, describing a typical weekend. "Last Sunday it was terribly hot. I played a lot of tennis and I had 11 relatives for dinner. Always sweating. Just did too much. Always had to change my clothes. Dug up a plant from a neighbor's property, planted it on my own place. Packing to leave, putting all these soaking wet clothes into a garbage bag because nothing would ever dry. My favorite blue pants, four of these wonderful Battaglia shirts in white, and a red blouse, and a few other things. And they were thrown out, along with the garbage bag. So I lost all my favorite clothes."

◆ On a mantel a wooden marksman fires over an elephant's tooth, one of the two that Kate brought back from Africa and the film location of THE AFRICAN QUEEN. The framed picture is a drawing Kate made in Central Park. An antique child's sled, original owner unknown, sits in a corner of the living room.

◆ All Hepburn residences are filled with strange things collected or received from friends. A stuffed duck flies over a toy soldier and a model ship. An African mask rests on an antique clock. In the main hall a barrel full of old canes and golf clubs stands in front of ancient skis and a friend's drawing of the Fenwick lighthouse.

◆ At the original Hepburn home at 133 Hawthorn Street in Hartford, the motto "Listen to the song of life" was inscribed on the fireplace and it is in needlepoint on this pillow in the Fenwick living room. An antique duck, porcelain bowl, and jewelry in one room, an old carved seagull in another.

◆ She prepares to load the car after the weekend. "I do the flowers; they travel from New York to Connecticut and back."

◆ The artifacts-filled living room at Fenwick.

◆ Though she no longer golfs, she drives around Fenwick in a cart director George Cukor gave to her in their MGM days.

◆ On her favorite chair on the sun deck, she studies one of the countless books and scripts that flow in constantly.

◆ Overleaf: As if in a scene from THE AFRICAN QUEEN, Kate steers her canoe through the rushes only a few hundred yards from the front door of her house. "This isn't a dream, it's Fenwick … or is it Paradise?" she asks.

◆ Kate visits her oldest and dearest friend, Laura Harding, at Laura's country place in Holmdel, New Jersey. They have known each other since they were aspiring actresses in New York, attending Mrs. Robinson-Duff's famous voice classes.

Says Laura, an American Express heiress, "I met her in 1928. I first thought, 'She's not my type. We'd never like each other.' Isn't that funny? She had long hair pulled back in a knot, a man's sweater pinned at the back with a big safety pin—what we called a 'Brooks sweater'— and a tweed skirt.

She always rushed impetuously into class." Later, after summer stock and Broadway, Kate was summoned to Hollywood for her first film. On July 1, 1932, Kate boarded the train in Ossining and Laura boarded in New York for the four-day trip to Pasadena, where the stars always debarked because it was closer

to Beverly Hills than Los Angeles's Union Station. They were met by her agents, Leland Hayward and Myron Selznick, who escorted them to a yellow Rolls-Royce for the ride into Hollywood. The Legend had begun.

◆ On September 9, 1989, Kate hosted her first wedding reception at the Fenwick house—for her friend Cynthia McFadden, a television producer, who was marrying Pulitzer Prize–winner Michael Davies, publisher of the HARTFORD COURANT. In preparation, author Scott Berg, another Hepburn friend, helps her take down porch screens.

◆ After the ceremony at the Fenwick church, the bridal couple walks to the house. Kate and her driver, Jimmy Davis, cart other guests by car.

❖ Overleaf: Cutting the cake under the big party tent that was attached to the front porch of the house.

◆ In the garden of a neighbor who is away Kate picks ripening berries so they will not go to waste. It was on the porch of this house, behind her, that she and her play-mates, later known as the Hepburn Players, put on their first theatrical.

◆ "Dick puts some sort of secret formula on his tomatoes to make them grow so beautifully."

◆ Kate and Phyllis prepare chicken pa-prika in the kitchen.

THERE are several discrepancies about her actual birth date ("Just use any of them," she says), but the birthday of 1989 saw her New York house so filled with flowers that she was sending them out to nursing homes and hospitals. One acquaintance sent seven dozen red roses with a card reading, "For Katie at 80, with a couple to spare."

She once said to NEWSWEEK that growing old has never bothered her much. "It ain't going to change, is it? The only thing I feel is that to play an old freak or an old jackass, or sit in a nursing home…well, that's not going to be interesting to anybody, especially the people in the nursing home. People should try to keep themselves as mobile as they can, but not with the terror of fighting a monster because then you have to say, 'Would you like to go on living forever?' I say, 'No, please. I'm not afraid to die. I think I'll just go to sleep.'"

Her energy never flags. At age 77, when most of her contemporaries were either dead or long retired, she wrote her first book, a 129-page memoir with the long title THE MAKING OF "THE AFRICAN QUEEN" OR HOW I WENT TO AFRICA WITH BOGART, BACALL AND HUSTON AND ALMOST LOST MY MIND. The book came into being when her close friend, Irene Selznick, whose autobiography had been published by Knopf, read some of the journal Kate keeps of her experiences and observations. She prevailed upon Kate to expand it and submit it to the same publisher, who snapped it right up.

The slim volume went almost immediately on the THE NEW YORK TIMES bestseller list. AFRICAN QUEEN director John Huston called from Malibu to say he loved it, and the critics raved. NEWSWEEK put her on the cover and excerpted the book. THE NEW YORK TIMES pontificated: "As a real veteran of the stage and screen, she possesses a perspective on the industry that few performers can rival. And today her views on film are informed by her characteristic feisty reverence for common sense, integrity and good taste."

Because of her book's success, she has begun writing, in longhand on yellow legal pads, her autobiography. "I'll never do the kind of book that people try to do on me," she says, "but what a person has learned from life is interesting to me."

"I've written about things everyone experiences," she says, "success, failure, sickness, moving out of a house you love, and smashing up a car. But I'm not going to write anything about my deep personal life. I don't understand why people care about things like that. I mean I'm sure you've slept with one or two people, too, if that's your sport, and I certainly don't want to hear about it. So why would anyone be interested in whom I've been to bed with?"

◆ **The force of nature never stops. After dinner, she does dishes and prepares for tomorrow's meals. Then she will go upstairs and read or write.**

◆ The house is filled with antiques, knick-knacks, sculptures, carvings, paintings and drawings (many by Kate, mostly unsigned), and other beloved items gathered over a life-time. Old childhood ice skates hang in the front hall, and the beam of an early boat is suspended from the living-room ceiling. Though she denies any connection, the dining-room chande-lier, covered with veils, is strangely reminiscent of Kate in her veils in THE AFRICAN QUEEN. "Brother Dick's lamp. He put it together," says Kate.

◆ In the dining room she is surrounded by a museum of artifacts she brought back from a jungle location. "Treasures from AFRICAN QUEEN. I'm sitting on a chief's chair. See the mask, the oar, the stool."

In her book on the making of THE AFRICAN QUEEN, she described her costar, Humphrey Bogart. "To put it simply: there was no bunk about Bogie. He was a man.... A generous actor. He just did it. He was an actor who enjoyed acting. Knew he was good. Always knew his lines. Always was on time. Liked to play with a hat or cap on – something – anything on. That damned hairpiece.... He was an extraordinarily decent fellow...."

◆ Kate peers through the door of Patrick's Country Store in Old Saybrook, her favorite place to shop. "Patrick's is closed on Sundays. A disappointment. As you can see, I need a new pair of pants."

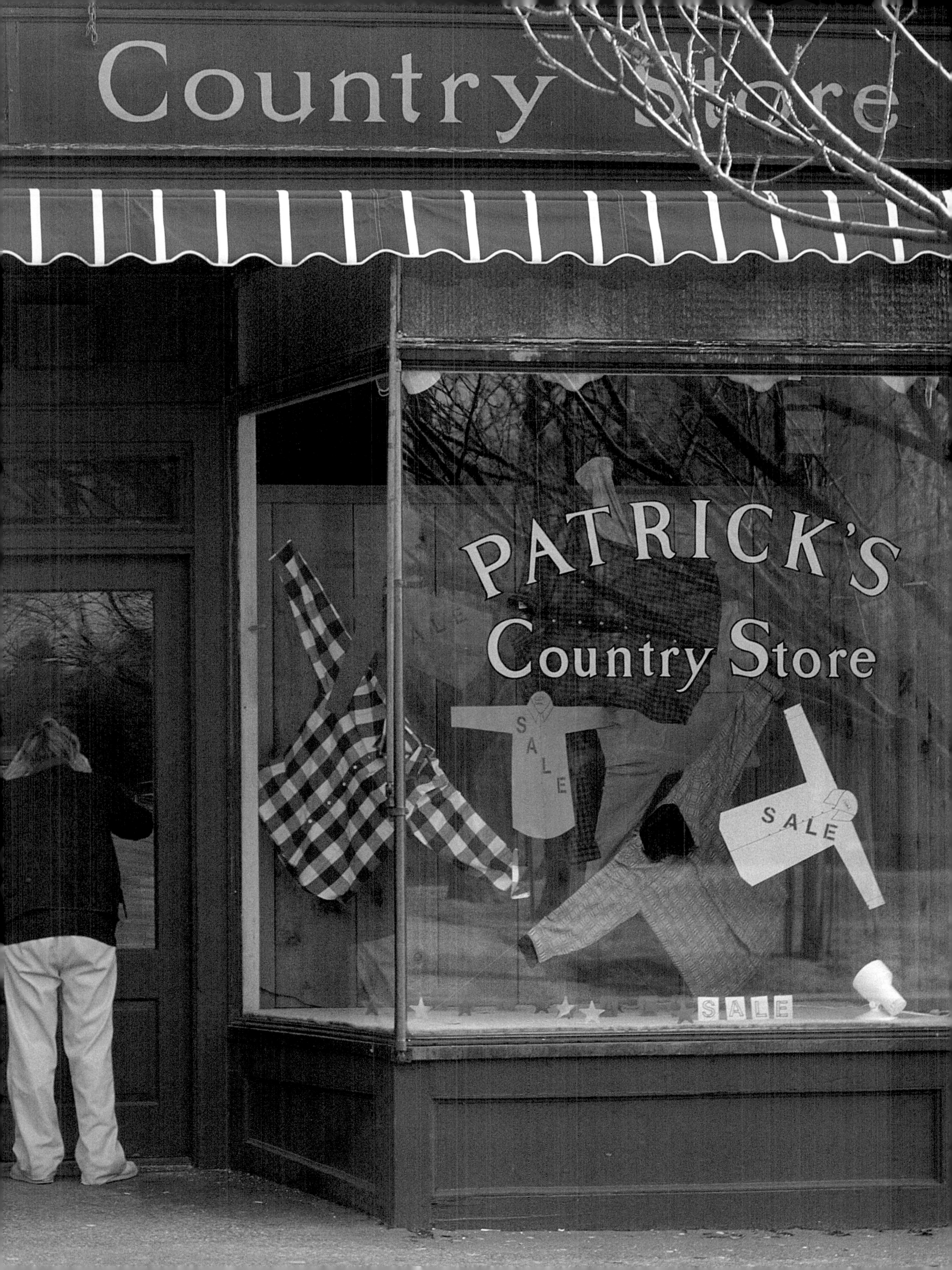
Country Store
PATRICK'S
Country Store
SALE
SALE
SALE

◆ In her bedroom, some of her paintings and art collection and a rattan rocking horse given to her years ago by a friend, the great English actress Constance Collier.

◆ In another corner
of the bedroom,
part of the Hepburn
hat collection. "A hat
for each picture,"
says Kate.

◆ In her bedroom at Fenwick, she studies a script. Says Kate: "Paradise to me is getting up at four-thirty or five o'clock in the morning. The house is absolutely quiet and I'll have a big roaring fire and I'll just stay in bed and have a great big breakfast: bacon, chicken livers, steak and eggs, that kind of food. And orange juice and a big pot of coffee. Then I just stay in bed and do my script reading or my writing or whatever I have to do. Then I watch the sun rise. From December 21 to June 21, right to left, you'll see a sunrise in each window as the months pass. Oh, golly, Paradise."

◆ Overleaf: Outside the house at Fenwick, she relaxes under the trees.

ENWICK IN MID-FEBRUARY. Kate emerges from her morning dip in Long Island Sound, tiptoeing across the ice and snow. The thermometer outside the kitchen door registers 5 degrees, and brother Dick reports the windchill is 20 degrees below zero. She has been making these swims since she was five. "Not everyone is lucky enough to understand how delicious it is to suffer," she says. It is part of the old Yankee tradition handed down from her father. In warm weather she takes an ice-cold shower each morning.

Working with the Duke

◆ **Early morning, on location in Oregon, director Stuart Millar goes over lines with Kate and Duke Wayne as the cameras are being set up.**

◆ **At the lunch break, instead of eating in the overcrowded mess tent, Kate has a private picnic on her own linens in a nearby copse. The meal includes cheeses, fruit, corn chips, and the inevitable thermos of cold soup. "You call this working?"**

◆ **Overleaf: A crew member helps her move her full-length mirror so it will not be in the next shot. It goes everywhere she goes. " If I don't look right," she says, "it's my fault."**

Word went out in the fall of 1974 that Katharine Hepburn and John Wayne were converging on a film location in the lovely Cascade Mountains and the deserts of Oregon to begin filming Rooster Cogburn.

She held the record as a three-time Oscar winner and Duke Wayne was possibly the top box-office money-earner in film history. (He was to play his Rooster Cogburn character from the smash hit True Grit, which got him his first Oscar.)

There was a complex chemistry at work. Everyone knew that Hepburn had espoused liberal causes throughout her long career, and Wayne was probably the most vocal political reactionary since the term was coined. Socially, she was a proper Yankee lady and Duke Wayne was one of the great carousers of all time. To top it off, Hepburn was widely regarded as an artist and sophisticate, and Wayne was admired for playing a rough cowboy in some of Hollywood's best Western classics. It was nonetheless a match made in heaven, and wise veteran producer Hal Wallis, who produced True Grit and other films that, together, had garnered 32 Academy Awards, was wise indeed in bringing these two legends together in front of the lens for the first time.

It all began on September 5 and continued for 43 shooting days. From the first day until the last, it was a remarkable professional love affair between the two disparate stars. As one veteran crew member observed, "Goddam, there ain't nothing like a couple of old pros when they get going...."

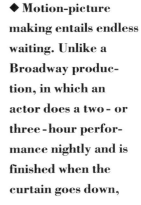

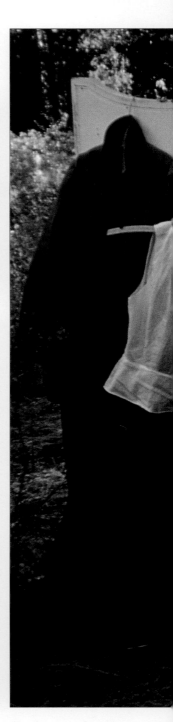

◆ Motion-picture making entails endless waiting. Unlike a Broadway production, in which an actor does a two- or three-hour performance nightly and is finished when the curtain goes down, movies require infinitely more. Takes, retakes, reverses, long shots, overalls, close-ups, rehearsals, and many second thoughts on how something can be done better.

In a wood out of sight of the film company, Kate studies her script and awaits the call to action.

She frequently writes in her journal. Soon, however, a respectful young assistant director, full of awe, will materialize and murmur, "Miss Hepburn, they're ready on the set."

◆ Overleaf: The place chosen for today's shots is two miles from the road. She could be ferried up in a camera truck or a four-wheel drive, but Kate prefers the walk through the woods.

◆ Kate gives the Duke some instructions. "Goddamn, she's a great dame," he bellowed into one Oregon night toward the end of the shooting. "She reminds me of me."

◆ "He'd look at me doing my own riding and he'd say, 'She's on there by the grace of God himself.'"

◆ Preceding pages: To film a conversation, the camera crew does close-ups of one actor speaking, while off-camera someone feeds the lines. Then, the entire scene is reshot with another performer speaking. When the film is cut, the alternating close-ups give the conversation a visual continuity. There are some stars who allow minions to feed their lines. Not so the first team. Here, John Wayne stands beside the camera giving the lines to Hepburn, who will reciprocate when the Duke's close-ups are being shot.

◆ Between shots on location, Kate chats with longtime friend Hal Wallis, who also produced TRUE GRIT.

◆ The camera boat, with crew aboard, is lashed to the raft that will carry the stars downstream, dodging shot and shell from the bad guys on the cliffs above.

HEPBURN ON DUKE, afterwards: "John Wayne. Amazing character. Good actor. Of course, he was a terrible reactionary. But funny. And fair. He had tiny Irish feet. About that long, you know, size eight and a half. Enormous man. Tiny feet. Big hands. You leaned against him and it was exactly like leaning against an oak tree."

◆ **The rapport between the two old professionals is profound, but they cannot shake off the perhaps unconscious habits of a lifetime. They politely elbow each other off the screen, each upstaging the other, as the crew watches with fascination. A lifted eyebrow, a scratch, a move in the background, a pirouette turn, a nodding head as the other speaks, even a stolid stillness and silence that denotes enormous strength to the camera eye. All done with great respect and affection and afterwards, at "That's a cut," no theatrical hugs and kisses, but great roars of laughter.**

JUST ABOVE SUNSET

O N JUNE 10, 1967, Spencer Tracy died in the kitchen of the little guest house on George Cukor's Beverly Hills estate, on Doheny Drive just above Sunset Boulevard. Katharine Hepburn found him.

Over the years, Tracy had occupied the house, and after his death, Kate continued to live there when she was working in California.

The house was midway between the motion picture studios of Culver City, Hollywood, and the San Fernando Valley. She could drive to work easily and she could also take long walks nearby in the valleys and hills of neighboring Coldwater Canyon. Indeed, the custodians of the walled-in Franklin Canyon reservoir surreptitiously presented her with a key to the gate, so she could hike without being disturbed by fans wanting autographs and photos.

For many years after Tracy's death, good friend George Cukor kept the house as it had been in happier days, and when Kate came west for a film she would rent it.

"I would never buy a house in California," she says. "I rented all the time. I would go out there, make a picture, then come right back. I'm a Connecticut person and so I always come back to Connecticut."

◆ "I've lived with perfect freedom," she says. "I've lived like a man. I've got my own house. I live alone. Always have. So I haven't lived like a woman at all. I can mend anything, do all the tough work in the house, in the garden. Men have got it easy. They have got it really easy. They don't even have to support women anymore. I would not change anything I have done."

◆ Overleaf: Out on the patio, she studies still another script among the sweet peas.

The last Tracy-Hepburn film, GUESS WHO'S COMING TO DINNER, was finished only two weeks before Tracy died in this house.

The picture was the first big-star screen vehicle to deal with interracial marriage and was made against great odds. Tracy and Hepburn play a socialite WASP couple whose daughter, played by Kate's niece, Katharine Houghton, falls in love with a black Rhodes scholar and UN consultant, Sidney Poitier, and wants to marry him.

Because of the subject matter, and Tracy's health, Columbia Pictures insisted that both stars put up their salaries in lieu of the insurance money and work for percentages. Says Kate: "Spence worked very, very hard, after all those years of wondering why, what, who, when...."

Tracy gave his last performance. Though his character was originally opposed to the idea of his daughter marrying a black man, his prospective son-in-law wins him over and the speech against racial intolerance that he delivers in the final scene had enormous impact when the film was released.

GUESS WHO'S COMING TO DINNER was a big hit and made millions for Columbia. Kate has never seen the picture.

◆ **Tracy's desk, and Hepburn in the office amid Tracy memorabilia. As she sits in the office under the big carved goose she gave to Tracy, she says, "Spencer's bird, his Vlaminck, his friend, and his desk in his California house." After Cukor's death, the house was sold.**

◆ The Hepburn
fire burns, as always,
even in Southern
California.

◆ Working on her
journal in the living
room.

WALES

YOUNG DIRECTOR George Cukor cast the stage actress Katharine Hepburn, then in her early twenties, in her first film role, and they made nine motion pictures together over the next 50 years.

Of her first screen test, Cukor once remembered, "It was quite unlike any test I had ever seen before. Though she'd never made a movie, she seemed to have this very definite knowledge and feeling right from the start."

The studio was appalled. Said producer David O. Selznick, "When Hepburn first appeared on our RKO lot there was consternation. 'Ye Gods, that horse face,' they cried, and when the first rushes were shown the gloom around the studio was so heavy you could cut it with a knife."

Cukor prevailed. That first film, A BILL OF DIVORCEMENT, starring John Barrymore, was a hit, and Katharine Hepburn was a movie star.

Forty-six years later, Hepburn and Cukor convened in the little village of Isybyty-Ifan, Wales, to put the Emlyn Williams play THE CORN IS GREEN on film for television. The two were by then old chums. She was delighted with the role of the Welsh school-teacher. "Oh, indeed, a wonderful part. My, I laughed and I cried and cried. Lovely for me. A woman alive. Not half dead."

◆ **"Oh George, how could you?" Outside a pub in the Welsh village of Isybyty-Ifan, the two old pals, Hepburn and Cukor, exchange knee slappers.**

◆ Besides Isybyty-Ifan, the Cukor company also worked in the town of Wrexham and the old Bersham colliery. Hepburn traipsed the Welsh countryside and, for authenticity, went down 1,300 feet through a narrow tunnel into a mine, carrying a lamp and gas detector and wearing a gas mask.

◆ Kate talks to British locations expert and art director Carmen Dillon, who spent months finding the right places to shoot.

◆ At another location, she shares a laugh with the camera crew and English cinematographer Ted Scaife.

◆ **Overleaf: Resting between takes outside his trailer, director Cukor murmurs to** **the photographer: "Reverence, please, Miss Hepburn is studying her script."**

◆ As Kate walks from her trailer to the camera setup, local ladies who are working as extras on the film give her a close perusal.

◆ She exchanges views on acting with British actor Bill Fraser, who plays the squire.

◆ Though Warner Brothers and CBS suggested tactfully, through the producers, that it might be best for the 69-year-old leading lady to allow a stunt woman to ride the heavy 1890 bicycle across the rough roads of the Welsh countryside, the indomitable Kate jumped aboard, pedaled with gusto, and exclaimed, "Downhill or on the flats, please not up...."

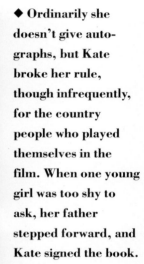

◆ Ordinarily she doesn't give autographs, but Kate broke her rule, though infrequently, for the country people who played themselves in the film. When one young girl was too shy to ask, her father stepped forward, and Kate signed the book.

◆ Between shots, Kate frequently strolled through the rolling hills to indulge her penchant for plucking wildflowers.

THE TWO OLD PALS talked frequently during this last project together (Cukor died in 1983). Besides her first film role in A BILL OF DIVORCEMENT, he directed her in many classics—LITTLE WOMEN, HOLIDAY, THE PHILADELPHIA STORY, KEEPER OF THE FLAME, PAT AND MIKE—and cast her with Sir Laurence Olivier in LOVE AMONG THE RUINS for television.

Said Kate of George once in an interview: "He is obviously unique in my life. He presented me to the public in a way calculated to make me seem fascinating. He used very shrewdly what I had to offer: my harsh voice, which threw the sound department into despair (George said, 'Get it'); my skinny face ('Make it look fascinating'); my eccentric ways, eccentric then, the rule now (He made them seem like virtues).

"He is a romantic. He is stagestruck. He is a romantic about actors. Loves all their unique personalities. Puts up with their foolishness. Loves them, ridicules them, frees them, gets the best out of them because he gives them confidence in themselves. Try it, do it. Now do it again. Now do it faster. Keep it up. Get it going. Exciting! What I owe to him."

Force of Nature

THE SPORTING LIFE

Katie at 80: "I believe in violent exercise," she says. "I used to play tennis three hours a day, and I was a very good golfer, even when I was a kid. But I can't golf now because I've got a very bad back, and golf requires a snap. I still swim a lot. I take long, brisk walks straight uphill or through the woods where you have to crawl or bend or climb over fences."

It is not always easy. She is still recuperating from two operations on her right ankle, so severely fractured in an automobile accident in 1982 near the Fenwick house that doctors thought her foot would have to be amputated. It always hurts, particularly in cold weather. "The thing's still swollen, but it works," she says. "And I've got the foot instead of its being in a hospital garbage can."

A few years ago, she began to exhibit slight tremors in some of her film work, and there were rumors that she was ill. Now, she feels compelled to explain publicly that her "shakes," as she calls them, are not Parkinson's disease but a nervous tic inherited from her grandfather and brought on by working too long hours. "Whiskey does the trick," says the former abstainer, who now occasionally has a shot before bed. "They stop completely if you drink enough," she says. "Of course, so does everything else."

◆ Tennis remains a passion, and she plays daily at Fenwick. "If there is a heaven," she announces, "and if that's where I end up, and if I'm a tennis champion – then I'll be happy."

◆ On the Fenwick tennis court, not far from her house, she plays a hard game, though it has slowed some since the automobile accident. "If I can't get to the ball in time," she says, "I'm allowed to have any number of bounces."

Here, she works out with young Kevin Conroy, the Fenwick tennis pro.

In New York, a man comes to her house every day. "I do exercises with him and get a massage. I also stand on my head for four minutes."

◆ Preceding pages: Wherever there is water, she swims. "I'm a tremendous believer in water, think it cures all ills," she says. "I swim every day of every weekend in Long Island Sound, summer and winter." Here, during the filming of ON GOLDEN POND in New Hampshire, she takes her daily dip in Squam Lake.

◆ Phyllis, driver L. C. Fischer, and Kate get the bike ready for a ride in Central Park. Kate: "Just tie it down." Phyllis: "I think it would be safer to tie you down, Miss Hepburn."

Kate used to bicycle from her house to the park, but traffic got too heavy and too many people recognized her at stoplights.

◆ She stops to rest at a favorite place overlooking the Central Park Lagoon. She has been going to a special spot nearby, surrounded by bushes, since she was a young ingenue. "There is a place in the park," she says, "where the rock is wonderfully shaped. A lot of tramps (I'm one of them) have discovered that if you line this crevice with newspapers, you can lie there in the middle of winter and the sun bakes down and it's absolutely delicious. Many's the part I have studied there."

One day a stranger walked up, looked down at her, and said, "Miss Hepburn, I've wanted your autograph for years." As always, Kate refused. The man walked away without his autograph, but stopped after about 30 feet and said, "Thanks, anyway, Audrey."

◆ On a Sunday at the Old Saybrook harbor, Kate helps brother-in-law Ellsworth Grant carry the dinghy to the water. They will row out to the Grant sailboat, *LADY FENWICK*.

◆ On the pier, Kate and her sister Marion (who died in 1987) load the rowboat with a picnic lunch for the day's sail on Long Island Sound.

◆ **Overleaf: The family rows the dinghy out in North Cove to the waiting *LADY FENWICK*.**

◆ "I see a mast. I pose. I am an actress."

◆ **Kate plunks down in the best seat on the boat: "Trust me to find my spot!"**

◆ Ellsworth, a former mayor of West Hartford, unwraps the sails. He lives a few doors from Kate in Fenwick and is the family film custodian. In addition to a large library of Kate's motion pictures and television shows, he also has all of the family's 16mm home movies that Kate's husband, Luddy, took. Kate, usually averse to watching her own films, saw some of them, such as THE AFRICAN QUEEN, for the first time in Ellsworth's screening room.

◆ Marion makes ready with the bow line as the family returns home at the end of the day.

Very Legitimate

ON THE BOARDS

◆ **At rehearsals for A MATTER OF GRAVITY with Wanda Bimson and a then relatively unknown young actor, Christopher Reeve, on his way to becoming Superman.**

KATE HEPBURN'S first theatrical effort was on the porch of a neighbor's house in Fenwick. She and some of the neighborhood kids put on a performance of BEAUTY AND THE BEAST to buy a Victrola for Navajo Indian children far, far away on the reservation. She was the Beast.

These amateur theatricals led to the formation of the Hepburn Players. But her first professional job, in the summer after graduating from Bryn Mawr, was a small role in THE CZARINA, which ran for a week in Baltimore. "Good notices," Kate says.

In early 1974, she began rehearsals in New York for A MATTER OF GRAVITY, her 25th play. She had behind her such major successes as THE PHILADELPHIA STORY (415 Broadway performances, 254 on the road), COCO, and eight Shakespearean dramas. Even so, she described her pain as a stage performer. "I like to go to bed early so I can get up early," she said. "That's why I love the movies, because they begin working so early. And that's why the theater is an agony for me, be-

cause by the time I finish the show and unwind, it's almost 1:30 A.M. Those hours are so alien to me. I feel like a jailbird."

She continues to view acting askance: "Today they do a great deal of ACTING all in capitals," she has said. "There's too much talk about it—and if I see the wheels going around in an actor's head or if it's too visibly worked upon, it's exhausting."

"Never forget," she told another critic, "that they don't give a Nobel Prize for it, and that Shirley Temple was doing it perfectly adequately at the age of four."

◆ Curtain calls at out-of-town tryouts for A MATTER OF GRAVITY at the Colonial Theatre in Boston.

◆ Overleaf: In WEST SIDE WALTZ Kate played a crippled piano teacher. Although the actual musical notes were piped into the theater and no one in the audience could see her keyboard, Hepburn insisted on learning to approximate the music so her finger movements would be correct. Here, at home, she practices with pianist and longtime friend Laura Fratti. Says Kate, "If the music goes up and your hands go down, it's embarrassing. Laura taught me fingering for WEST SIDE WALTZ. The hardest task I ever faced."

◆ After a sellout three-month tour around the country, Kate and the cast of WEST SIDE WALTZ rehearse in the ANTA Theater in New York before the Broadway opening. "I've been frightfully lucky, I'd say. I was lucky to get this play. I'm lucky to have been able to continue as long as I have. It gets more complicated, though. The older you get, the more intelligent you get, so the more aware you are of where you're rotten. You're much more aware of the audience and their hopes and your own hopes...."

As the rehearsals continue, Kate plays Chopin waltzes for costar Dorothy Loudon, on violin, and the rest of the cast.

◆ During a long
afternoon's rehearsal
in the darkened
theater, Hepburn and
director Noel Wilman
give a young actress a
quick course in stage
manners. Perhaps
Kate's mind flits back
nearly 50 years to
1932, when she was
an aspiring young
thespian.
Director (to young
actress): "You moved
on Miss Hepburn's
line...and if you keep
doing it, she will kill
you and I will
provide her with an
alibi."
Hepburn: "Or an
axe."
Young Actress: "I
wish you'd tell me
when to move...."
Hepburn: "Never
move on other
people's jokes."

ABOUT TRACY

NEWSWEEK: *"Of Hollywood love stories that put our current Age of the Bimbo to shame, the very private 27-year partnership she formed with Spencer Tracy is surely the finest."*

EVEN THOUGH there were tabloids and Hollywood gossip columnists like Louella and Hedda and a plenitude of paparazzi during the 27 years they shared their lives together, unmarried, the media left superstars Katharine Hepburn and Spencer Tracy pretty much alone.

The bedeviled, hard-drinking Tracy anguished over his Catholic faith and did not divorce his wife. From their first on-screen pairing in 1942 in WOMAN OF THE YEAR, he and Hepburn made nine big pictures together. Their romance was Hollywood legend. He called her "Kathy," or "Kath," never "Kate." Sometimes "Ratty."

They were motion picture nobility, but they never went out together to restaurants, movie premieres, or big parties. They maintained separate residences and the press honored their privacy.

"I never went out in public with Spencer, never, ever did. Ever," says Kate. "Mrs. Tracy lived in California and he was married to Mrs. Tracy and I didn't think it was my place to be seen all over town with him. The press respected it for the reason that I respected it and Spencer respected it. We went out of our way to be reticent. And I think people thought, 'Well, if it means that much to them, let's shut up.'"

Two weeks after finishing their last film, GUESS WHO'S COMING TO DINNER, Tracy died of a heart attack in the little guest house at George Cukor's Beverly Hills estate; Kate found him in the kitchen, slumped before a cup of tea he had been making. Through the years she had maintained a distance from the Tracy family affairs; she did not attend the funeral. "I felt I might be in the way," she said.

In the years that followed, she plunged into her work in films and on the stage, all around the world, and always maintained a discreet silence on the great love of her life.

In 1986, 19 years after Tracy's death, Hepburn astonished the world when she agreed to host a 90-minute PBS documentary for television entitled THE SPENCER TRACY LEGACY: A TRIBUTE BY KATHARINE HEPBURN. She gathered such costars and friends as Frank Sinatra, Elizabeth Taylor, Joan Bennett, Angela Lansbury, Lee Marvin, Mickey Rooney, Robert Wagner, Joanne Woodward, Richard Widmark; directors Stanley Kramer, Joseph Mankiewicz, and John Sturges; and Tracy's daughter, Susie. She also visited locations where they had worked together and she showed film clips of some of his greatest screen moments.

◆ In her home in New York, she stands in front of her favorite portrait of Spencer Tracy. "He's just ever present."

◆ Overleaf: During the filming of the Tracy documentary, she visits with Tracy's daughter, Susie, at her home next to Brentwood's Riviera Country Club. Tracy played polo with his cronies here, and Tracy and Hepburn did scenes for their film PAT AND MIKE here.

Her tribute to Spencer Tracy was an enormous success and has been reshown many times.

"He was elemental," she said, "air, fire, water, earth. A hugely complex man from whose tangled center there emerged an absolute truth and simplicity of acting."

Speaking of him, after many years of silence, she remembers the hard-working, hard-living, extremely talented Tracy.

On acting: "I knew his work and admired it passionately. I think he was a brilliant actor from beginning to end. It's all based on the same simplicity. It wasn't a type of acting; it was taking the material and playing it...just being....

"I don't think he thought, 'Oh, I'm an actor, that's the greatest thing in the world.' He always used to say, 'Remember who killed Lincoln.' With humor, of course, everything was with humor."

Working together: "We never rehearsed the scene we were going to do together. It's so hard to know why you do get on with one person and not another. That's a very subtle thing. Oh, the enormous complication of the human being. It's extraordinary, I think. And also thrilling.

"Spence had a remarkable memory. He was the quickest study I've ever seen in my life. Spence could read a page and then could tell you every idea in that page. The most extraordinary concentration that I've ever seen.

"To me, his acting was the real stuff that life is made of, his world and his reality instead of the fancy box with nothing in it. I shall never forget when we finished making SEA OF GRASS and the crew gave us each a present. I spoke first and went on and on about how gorgeous it was. Then Spencer stood up, looked around at everyone (he was very moved at what they had

given him), and said, 'Thank you. Thank you very, very much.' Well, I died. And that was the way he acted."

The man: "Spence saw many things invisible to others. Fascinating to be with. He had a terrific sense of tragedy and an exquisite, sort of wounded sense of laughter. He could see through sham. Yes, he was a fine friend to me. Grew me up beyond my potential. Acting was his easiest thing. I mean, to him it was a relaxation.

"Living was never easy for Spence, he was deeply troubled. Not at all like that totally confident figure the public saw up there on the screen. But whatever it was that made him so unhappy, he never talked about it. Not with me, not to anyone. I realize now that I never really knew him.

"He was never happy just being Spencer. I don't think he liked himself very much. Acting must have been a relief for him, pretending he was someone else.

"He had a drinking problem, no doubt about it. His drinking was no problem between us. Drinking is your own problem, and the only person who can do anything about it is you. I admired Spencer for his ability to just stop. Spencer was amazing. He never went to Alcoholics Anonymous, yet would quit with a case of bourbon in the cupboard, and he wouldn't touch another drop for two or three years."

The relationship: "Let's just say that where change was required, I adjusted. In every relationship that exists, people have to seek a way to survive. If you really care about the person, you do what's necessary, or that's the end. For the first time I found that I really could change, and the qualities I most admired in myself, I gave up. I stopped being loud and bossy. Oh, all right, I was still loud and bossy, but only behind his back."

◆ In her home, Tracy's daughter, Susie, shows Kate his diary. He made entries every day, always beginning with the date, the weather, and his weight that morning. One entry, for the day they began their first film together, says simply, "WOMAN OF THE YEAR, Katharine Hepburn."

◆ In the Thalberg Building at MGM she looks at the famous photograph taken for LIFE of all the MGM stars in one picture. She is the only actress wearing slacks.

OUTSIDE the main entrance to MGM, she remembers exactly where she was when she met Tracy. "I was on my way into this building," she says, "and it was just about here that Spencer and I first met. He and producer Joe Mankiewicz were on their way to the commissary. Joe said it was about time we met. We were to do WOMAN OF THE YEAR.

"Now Spencer wasn't short, by any means, but in those days I was considered rather tall, five seven and a half, plus my heels. So I said, 'I hope it doesn't bother you that I'm so tall. I'm wearing heels, but I can change them.'

"Spencer gave his impenetrable smile.

It was Joe who replied, 'Don't worry, Kate, he'll cut you down to size.'"

Toward the end of filming the PBS documentary, she was seized one night with a feeling that she had to write to Tracy. In a few minutes, she wrote a four-page letter, then agonized for days whether she should read it on the air. Finally, this most private of women decided it would "give people a true sense of the man."

In one passage, she speaks of his drinking. "Why the escape hatch? Why was it always opened to get away from that remarkable you? What was it, Spence? I meant so to ask you. Did you know what it was? What did you say? I can't hear you...."

◆ Metro-Goldwyn-Mayer was the "studio of the stars," and its main gate was for decades the most important portal in the motion-picture world. Standing at this place through which she and Tracy and all of the major stars passed each day on their way to work, she mused, "It looks so sad now, as if it knows what is going to happen to it." She was right. Shortly thereafter, the proud old MGM lot became Lorimar (primarily a television film company), and now it has become the studio of Columbia Pictures (owned by Sony).

KATE & HANK...
"IT'S ABOUT TIME"

THERE are discrepancies about the first meeting of Katharine Hepburn and Henry Fonda. By 1979, she had worked with most of the great male film stars: Spencer Tracy, Humphrey Bogart, James Stewart, Cary Grant, John Wayne, Frederic March, John Barrymore, Charles Boyer, Robert Mitchum, Burt Lancaster, Montgomery Clift, Laurence Olivier, Peter O'Toole. But it wasn't until they were cast together in ON GOLDEN POND that she met Henry Fonda.

Says director Mark Rydell: "It was our first day on the set and when I heard they hadn't been introduced I was astonished; after all, they represented a hundred years of movie making. So I took Kate onto the set and I said, 'Miss Hepburn, this is Mr. Henry Fonda,' and he just said, 'About time, too.'"

Fonda recalled the meeting in a cover story TIME did on the two when the hit film opened. Fonda said he was in a 20th Century-Fox soundstage basement when "Kate just came in, smiled, looked directly at me, and said, 'It's about time.'"

Asked for a verification, Hepburn laughs and says, "Why don't you use both, it's terribly amusing."

◆ On location in New Hampshire, the camera crew photographs the two stars in a gazebo on Squam Lake.

◆ Between takes, Hepburn takes long walks through the woods surrounding her location home.

◆ The film crew clambers aboard a camera boat to accompany Kate and Hank on an action sequence as he chauffeurs her around the lake.

◆ In a later scene, insisting as always on doing her own stunt work, Kate starts and runs the outboard herself. She also does her own diving and swimming sequences.

◆ Her full-length mirror – accompanying her wherever she works on location – is erected in the New Hampshire forest.

◆ Filmmaking on location is enormously involved, and costly, but it gives the picture an authenticity that cannot be matched in a studio or on a soundstage. On Squam Lake, the camera crew sets up for a high shot; later, they photograph the stars from a camera boat; and finally, during a rainstorm, Kate gives a few suggestions to a stunt man overseeing the motorboat sequences.

◆ In a touching sequence in the film, Ethel (Hepburn) unveils a surprise birthday cake she has baked for Norman (Fonda) as their daughter, Chelsea (Jane Fonda), looks on. Says Kate, "Hank. What a darling man."

Said Henry of ON GOLDEN POND, his last motion picture: "I love Kate for playing with me in this film. Other movies have had a lot of meaning for me—GRAPES OF WRATH, THE OX-BOW INCIDENT, MISTER ROBERTS, 12 ANGRY MEN—but ON GOLDEN POND is the ultimate role in my career."

◆ The movie couple embraces. Said Fonda: "It was a magical summer for both of us. We worked together as though we'd been doing it all our lives. Kate is unique–in her looks, in the way she plays, most of all in herself. It was just the second time Kate and I met, that first morning on Squam Lake. People kind of melted away and there were just the two of us. She had this thing clutched in her hand and she held it out to me. 'For you,' she said. 'It was Spencer's favorite hat.' I wore it in the next scene."

That night, Fonda, who was a painter of delicate still lifes, was inspired to start a painting of the three hats he wore in the film. He gave the painting to Kate.

◆ Though the film company provides her choice of hairdressers (she has brought one from London), she takes care of her own hair after a long day in front of the cameras. A certain number of brushings, the rollers, the curlers, the pins, brushes, combs, all part of early lessons learned as a young actress. Kate explains, " These rolls of newspaper are all different sizes to make whatever size curl you want. The paper absorbs the water."

◆ Overleaf: Another day coming up on the set of ON GOLDEN POND. At four-thirty in the morning, while having her coffee, studying her script, and drying her freshly shampooed hair with a heat lamp, she observes, "I wish every aspiring young actress could see me like this."

◆ Between takes, Kate chats with Phyllis Wilbourn and her English hairdresser, Ray Gow.

◆ For a scene in the film, she touches up the Thayer mailbox.

◆ The stars' folding chairs for the film, carried everywhere by the prop man and set up wherever the cameras go. Real movie memorabilia. Film crew members have been known to fight for chairs like these after a picture is wrapped.

◆ Kate with costar Jane Fonda, who put the film together and was coproducer. "I've always thought of ON GOLDEN POND as a present to my father," Jane once said. "There's a lot of Dad in the part, and I guess there's a lot of Chelsea, Norman's daughter, in me....

There's a lot of love, I think you can see it on the screen. ON GOLDEN POND gave all of us the chance to say out loud some-thing you could admit to yourself only at night."

Said Jane, after the production wrapped, "I couldn't help fantasizing what would have happened if she and my dad had become lovers 40 years ago, and Kate had been my mother...."

◆ The two old pros demolish the film crew and, later, the audience: "Spence and Hank felt the same way I do," says Kate. "The camera sees through the performance. We were brought up in the school that teaches: You do what the script tells you. Deliver the goods without comment. Live it, do it – or shut up. The writer is what's important. If the script is good and you don't get in its way, it will come off okay. I never discussed a script with Spence; we just did it. The same with Hank in On Golden Pond. Naturally and unconsciously, we joined into what I call a 'musical necessity'– the chemistry that brings out the essence of the characters and the work."

◆ ON GOLDEN POND is a smash. As TIME magazine wrote: "There could have been trumpets, a heavenly choir, an enveloping cushion of fleece and lots of silver streamers – at least a few moguls and a newsreel camera. Someone important might have been there to introduce these two acting legends about to cross paths for the first time. 'Alice Adams meet Young Mr. Lincoln, Mary of Scotland, this is Wyatt Earp. Tracy Lord, Tom Joad, Tess Harding, Mister Roberts.'" Hepburn was awarded her fourth Oscar for the film. Henry's daughter, Jane, accepted his first Oscar and brought it home to his bedroom in Bel Air, where he died a few months later.

WORKING IN THE STREET

◆ **Between shots at a location next to New York's East River, Nick recovers under the sun, as his costar, shielded from it, smiles under her parasol.**

SHE'S A LEGEND, but once you get beyond that, she's just a cranky old broad who can sometimes be a whole lot of fun."

—NICK NOLTE, COSTAR

"I'm not nearly as cranky as I should have been with him…. He was getting drunk in every gutter in town."

—KATHARINE HEPBURN, COSTAR

"How can Miss Hepburn make a film like this? It's asinine."

—REX REED, FILM CRITIC

For more than 11 years, Hepburn had been wanting to make this film, ever since young writer Martin Zweiback had told her about it. She commissioned the script, but every studio in Hollywood turned it down as too macabre. Finally, she raised the money herself, hired old chum Anthony Harvey, who had directed her in THE LION IN WINTER, cast rising leading man Nick Nolte as costar, and her 43rd film, THE ULTIMATE SOLUTION OF

GRACE QUIGLEY, went before the cameras in the Bronx in 1984.

The film is an outrageous black comedy about an old woman (Hepburn), tired of life, who witnesses a murder in New York and blackmails the hit man (Nolte) into joining her in "a little business to bump off other aged people who wanted to die." Her aging clients are delighted with a quick way out of the slow descent into oblivion.

It was a subject she felt strongly about. "I think it is wicked to keep a hopeless life going through artificial methods," she says, adding that she has signed a "living will" that permits relatives and physicians to terminate her life under certain circumstances. "If I were just a 'thing' lying there and had to be kept alive by drip, drip, drip from a device, I would say, 'Take away the drip, please.' I think everyone should have the right to decide whether to live or die."

To critics of the subject matter she said, "One of the reasons I've weathered for as long as I have is that the topics I pick to do are interesting…. Everything you do has to show different aspects of your personality. You have to have a feeling for it. I was always playing myself in the movies, at least facets of myself."

GRACE QUIGLEY was not a success. "I liked the movie," said Kate, "but people couldn't stand it. I think it was the death angle. People are very sentimental about life and death. See, I look forward to life. I look forward to death. So I've got them fooled."

◆ **In a big scene from the film, Grace Quigley and her partner are entertained by their happy clients, who import a stripper for the party.**

◆ **Overleaf: Waiting for a call to the camera, Kate is interviewed by a team from the LOS ANGELES TIMES CALENDAR magazine.**

◆ The QUIGLEY com-
pany prepares to
shoot as Kate whis-
pers into her leading
man's ear. "Obviously
I'm telling him how to
play a scene," she
says. Director Har-
vey beams expec-
tantly. As always,
Hepburn's longtime
personal secretary,
Phyllis Wilbourn,
bundled against the
cold, watches over
every minute of the
actress's day.

◆ Between shots, Kate props up her feet and sits under her parasol to keep her delicate skin from reacting to too much sun. "The sun has absolutely ruined my skin," she says. "I have that awful kind of freckled, fair-skinned complexion that ought never be exposed to anything but fog…and a lot of people would say I already do live in a fog."

◆ Overleaf: As always, in the African jungle, the Oregon wilds, or the Bronx, Hepburn works on her makeup in the outdoors, rather than inside her trailer, since the scene will be filmed outdoors.

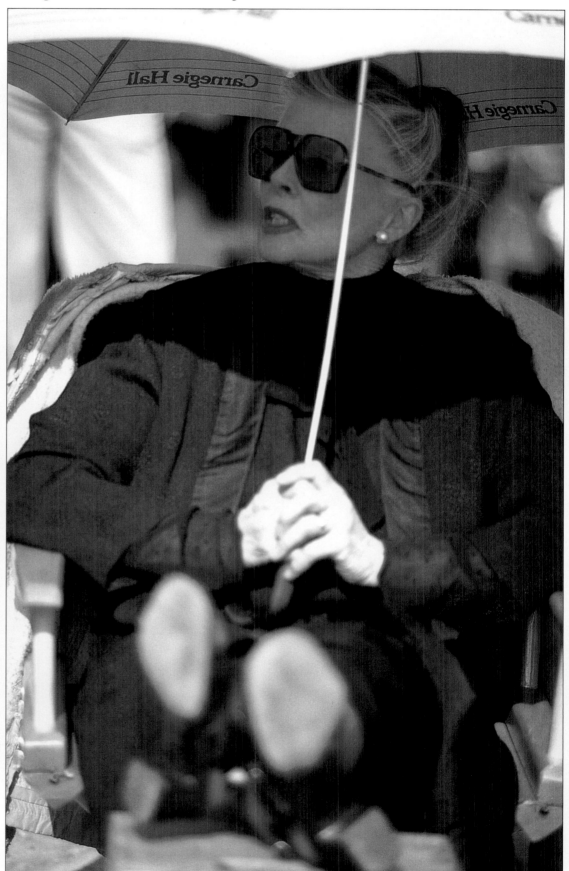

◆ **Asks Kate: "Did you ever ride a motorcycle with Nick Nolte driving? It's called 'risking.'"** Producers and film companies will do anything to keep featured stars from doing their own stunts. A sprained ankle running down stairs, a fall off a ladder, any incapacitating accident that can keep the star from working in front of the camera for an hour, a day, a week causes film accountants to sprout gray hair as they compute the added costs. When Hepburn, in her 70s, swings aboard Nick Nolte's motorcycle for a ride through the Bronx, strong men weep.

At Home in New York

SHE BEGAN TO RENT the house for $100 a month in 1931, when she was a young ingenue on Broadway. After she had hit the big time, in 1937, she bought the house for $27,000, and she recently turned down an offer of $2 million for it. "Best investment I ever made," she says.

It is a four-story brownstone in New York's Turtle Bay district, in an unusual block where the neighbors share a luxurious garden courtyard that is accessible only to residents. Homeowners can work the plots adjacent to their houses. There is an abundance of trees and greenery, and one's privacy and seclusion are carefully respected. Kate works in her garden winter and summer, and is sometimes observed by startled passersby as she shovels snow from the front of the house or unloads firewood from the trunk of her car.

Kate and staff frequently gather in the ground-floor kitchen, which is filled with good smells. There is also a large dining room that doubles as an office, the table piled high with a mountain of papers and fan mail. The entrance to the garden is down here, too. Says Kate: "I had a john put in on the ground floor because my mother reminded me that I should be considerate of my guests who reach a certain age."

◆ **When she returns from a weekend in Connecticut, she and longtime (17 years) housekeeper/cook Norah Moore unload firewood, cut by Kate herself, from the trunk of her car. "We cut 'em, we stack 'em, we burn 'em. It's our way of life."**

◆ **In her sitting room on the second floor, in her favorite chair, she confers with her niece, actress Kathy Houghton. She is the daughter of Kate's late sister, Marion.**

◆ **Overleaf: Kate and Kathy check rolls of fabric to re-cover some of the furniture in the sitting room. "Oh, no," says Kate. "White is the best color... then the flowers can supply the this's and that's."**

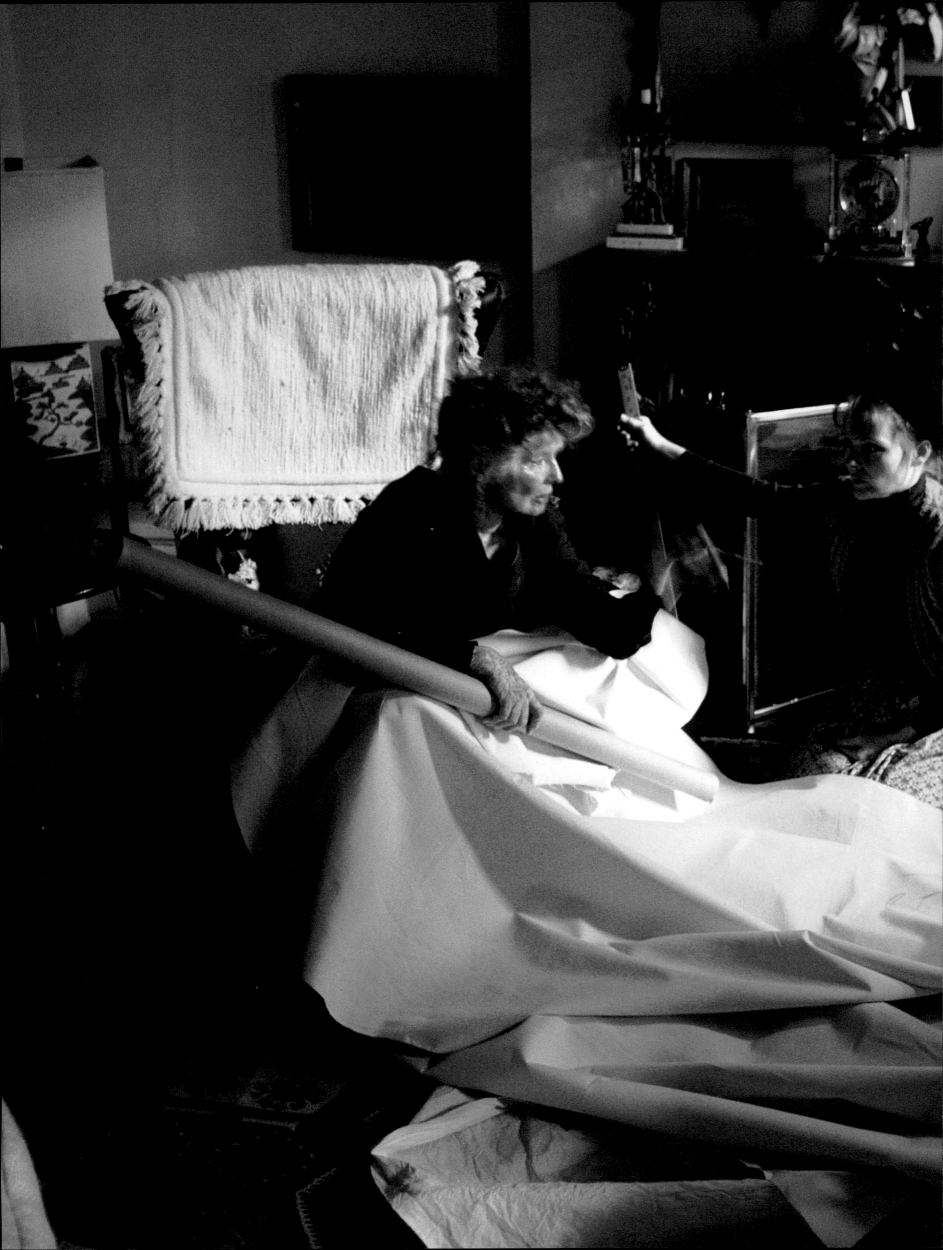

◆ Before dinner, drinks and old chum laughter in the living room with directors Anthony Harvey and Robert Helpmann. Harvey directed THE LION IN WINTER, Kate's third Oscar, and Bobby Helpmann took her to Australia for the Old Vic Company and a triumphant Shakespeare tour.

◆ In the living room, sitting in her favorite chair beneath Spencer's carved wooden goose, Kate works on her script for a television appearance she will make promoting birth control.

◆ Part-time and full-time staff gather to eat with Kate in the kitchen: hairdresser, makeup lady, secretary, and personal secretary. Madame ensconced on the kitchen couch, putting away Norah's famous soup.

◆ Overleaf: In the dining room, converted to office, Kate and secretary Sharon Powers attempt to deal with the flood of mail that arrives daily: fan letters, importunations, scripts, postcards from old friends, presents, personal notes.

Shaking her head at the pile, Kate laughs, "'Could you? Would you? My old mother? My young daughter? I hate to ask, but an autograph, or photograph, or book. Or could we meet?'"

The most treasured replies are handwritten notes on KATHARINE HOUGHTON HEPBURN stationery.

◆ **Preceding pages:
Kate wends her
way through New
York traffic on a
Monday morning,
coming back home
after a Connecticut
weekend.**

◆ **The Hepburn
Command Post in her
living room, next to
her favorite chair:
her magnifying glass,
phone, and chunks of
crystal, petrified
wood, cannonballs.
She always answers
the phone herself.**

◆ **In the study, a
Hepburn portrait by
Vancouver artist
Myfannwy Pavelick
Spencer and a rare
old bird. Carved,
cast, molded, and
stuffed, birds fill the
Hepburn households.**

◆ **The main Hepburn
New York fireplace,
which no one else is
ever allowed to tend,
is a private museum
of pre-Columbian
sculpture, antique
candleholders that
her father gave her,
more carved birds,
sculptures by Kate**

**and of Kate, sent by
friends and admirers,
and various dried
flowers. Says Kate:
"I love fireplaces,
Fenwick or New
York."**

◆ **More Hepburniana** *ad infinitum* **in the living room:** ANGEL ON A WAVE, **an original Kate Hepburn sculpture; atop the** fireplace, **a figure of Kate by sculptor friend Frances Rich and another bird; elsewhere around the room, an Eskimo** sculpture, **Kate as she appeared in the stage production of** ANTONY AND CLEOPATRA, **Martina Navratilova's winning racket from** Wimbledon, **and an original Hepburn painting,** GULLS ON THE ROCKS.

◆ The first photograph of the four Hepburn Oscars together. In 1933, in the early years of the Academy Awards, she won her first for MORNING GLORY. That first one is slightly smaller and more weather-beaten than the three big golden Oscars that she received for THE LION IN WINTER, GUESS WHO'S COMING TO DINNER, and ON GOLDEN POND. She was the first to win three Academy Awards and allowed the Guinness Hall of Records in New York to put them on permanent exhibition.

When she won her fourth Oscar, for ON GOLDEN POND, a friend who was very ill with cancer asked if he could borrow it for good luck. She loaned it to him, and he took it to the hospital in Boston. She later learned that the Oscar caused a great stir among the other patients and it inspired them all. His widow now has the statuette.

◆ A third-floor bedroom of the Turtle Bay house is devoted to wardrobe. Not a pair of high-heels in sight.

Though she once characterized herself as "the original bag lady," THE NEW YORK TIMES MAGAZINE recently ran a fashion story on her entitled HEPBURN STYLE. The article stated, "Katharine Hepburn is the essence of classic style."

Hepburn's comment is as classic as her style. "I'm very broad-shouldered, very long-armed, like a gorilla, so I always created a line that was comfortable, in other words, clothes that are too big."

She still wears the slacks that brought disapproval and even eyebrow-raising approbation during the thirties and forties; "Oh, in England, I'm sure they didn't think anything at all, the English being English," she says. "In California, I think they just thought I was queer."

◆ In her third-floor bedroom one early morning, Kate scribbles on yellow legal pads. ("I can't type; this is a set decoration," she says.) On the bureau is a picture of her father, some of her paintings are around the room, and on the table next to her is a photograph of Spencer Tracy and two of his polo ponies. "Beautiful head he has, hasn't he, inside and out," she says.

◆ Overleaf: Kate and niece Kathy Houghton, who sometimes stays with her, perambulating the Hepburn garden as they do the spring planting.

◆ Neighbors in nearby buildings have been known to invite guests out to the balcony and, handing them binoculars, impress them with, "That's Katharine Hepburn down there working in the garden."

◆ When spring burgeons, the busy Hepburn schedule is interrupted by daily calls to the plot outside.

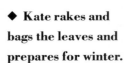

◆ Kate rakes and
bags the leaves and
prepares for winter.

◆ Overleaf: Turtle
Bay in winter,
shoveling snow off the
roof so it won't leak.

K ATE tells a story that has become
a Turtle Bay legend: "My next
door neighbor, the composer
Stephen Sondheim, was working
at the piano through many
nights on his score for A LITTLE NIGHT
MUSIC, and I nearly went mad. One night,
in a fury, I walked barefoot through the
snow in the backyard, just wearing my
pajamas, and pressed my face against the
window and looked in. I must have looked
like an old witch. He had a friend with
him, and they had drinks in their hands.
All of a sudden they both looked at me and
absolutely froze. I just stood there. Sec-
onds passed. They just stared at me. I
stared at them. I disappeared. Afterwards,
SILENCE."

ONCE UPON A TIME

ONE SUMMER MORNING in 1974, in Malibu, California, my telephone rang. It was John Loengard, the picture editor of LIFE, calling from New York.

The great weekly picture magazine had ceased publication several years before, but the wise editorial directors of Time Inc. had retained a skeleton staff to plan projects to keep the LIFE photojournalism tradition alive in the world.

Now, Loengard reported, they were planning a special issue, ONE DAY IN THE LIFE OF AMERICA, and he was assigning 100 of the best photographers in the country to cover the nation on September 5 to document every facet of life in the 50 states – the president, cowboys, writers, lovers, the old and young, sports figures, tragedies, the wilderness, everything.

Loengard said that Katharine Hepburn and John Wayne were on their way to a location in Oregon to do a Western film called ROOSTER COGBURN, and he wanted me to photograph the first day of shooting, September 5. I had never photographed either of these living legends and I was delighted. I arrived a day early to introduce myself to the principals and to explain the LIFE special project. Kate said only, "I hate to pose," and I assured her I wanted her in action and that posed pictures were the last thing I had in mind.

Wayne and I got on famously that evening, because of a mutual interest in Commerativo tequila.

The big day went well, with a fine action sequence on the Rogue River, and we got a big picture in LIFE. There was so much interest in the pair that I photographed a cover story on them several weeks later for PEOPLE. I also wrote the piece. It appears herewith, from the November 18 issue:

BEND, OREGON—It is 5 A.M., a morning so cold that first snow must be near. Cars move the cast and crew of ROOSTER COGBURN up into the pine forests of the Cascade range; then, an overland trek to a location so rugged that the usual portable toilets have not been brought in. Bushes serve.

It is the eighth week of shooting, and another 12-

hour day is just beginning. But the two sexagenarian stars of the film – John Wayne and Katharine Hepburn – have survived white-water raft rides, gallops across the desert and endless manhandling to emerge this morning, if possible, as fresh as when "Scene 1, Take 1" was called.

Wayne and Hepburn have never made a picture together before – though between them they have compiled 132 years of living, nine decades of filmmaking and almost 300 screen credits. In 47 years John Wayne has patented the image of the hard-to-anger but righteous Man of the West. For 42 years Hepburn has been honing her image as the feisty woman – but vulnerable to the right man – who will not be squelched.

Both of these screen images have been melded in ROOSTER COGBURN, which canny producer Hal Wallis created as a successor to the celebrated TRUE GRIT and to satisfy Hepburn's 18-year desire to "star in a western with Wayne." The Duke again limns the exploits of the one-eyed, whiskey-wallowing marshal that won him an Oscar. And Kate, herself a three-time Oscar recipient, plays Eula Goodnight, in essence the older sister of the snappish, spunky spinster she portrayed in THE AFRICAN QUEEN.

When shooting started their discreet sizing-up of each other was short-lived; soon he was calling her "Sister" and she was calling him "Duke." And they were dazzling the rest of the company with their on-camera chemistry and their assertiveness off it. "When two great monsters get together and begin working things out," Hepburn acknowledged with a smile, "it would be difficult for anyone." They were hardly monsters in most eyes. Crewmen are notoriously hardbitten; yet one wrangler said, "I cut my income in half to come up here – I just wanted to be part of it."

In between shots one day Duke was spinning a tall yarn. Hovering nearby, Kate – who once said "you shouldn't be a doormat" and has lived by that credo – sported the grin of a cheerleader hanging on to a high school quarterback's every word. Her smile, one crewman said, "takes 20 years off her face."

When a magazine photographer began to shoot the two stars as they prepared a scene, Kate shifted almost imperceptibly so a shaft of sunlight beamed through the trees onto her face. Duke tugged on one of his ears. The conversation continued, but Kate was not to be upstaged: she casually picked up a Winchester and began to load it.

Later that day they relaxed in conversation; and their viewpoints were strangely resonant:

On acting:

Kate: I think it's the most minor of gifts.

Duke: All I want instinctively is for the average guy to want to be in my shoes.

On sex:

Kate: The male sex, as a sex, does not universally appeal to me. I find the men today less manly: but a woman of my age is not in a position to know exactly how manly they are.

Duke: Everybody should do what's fun, but it's not a spectator sport.

On psychoanalysis:

Kate: Most of it is wild self-indulgence. The fact remains we're like those salmon – you know, you either get up the river or you don't.

Duke: I dive into cold water and everything looks a little different.

On each other:

Kate: He has confidence in himself, which gives him enormous charisma. He's quick, he's sensitive. He knows all the techniques. I think he's an awfully good actor – and a terribly funny man. We laugh all day. What a goddamn fascinating personality!

Duke: I have never in my life worked with a woman who had the smell of drama that this woman has. She is so feminine – she's a man's woman.

It was late at night. Two or three more days of shooting remained. Hepburn, as usual, had been in bed since 8. Wayne, as usual, had a bottle of Commemorativo tequila in front of him. "Imagine," he mused softly, "how she must have been at age 25 or 30 ... how lucky a man would have been to have found her." -J.B.